EMMANUEL JOSEPH

The Human Algorithm, Decoding Politics, Society, and Economics in the Modern World

Copyright © 2025 by Emmanuel Joseph

All rights reserved. No part of this publication may be reproduced, stored or transmitted in any form or by any means, electronic, mechanical, photocopying, recording, scanning, or otherwise without written permission from the publisher. It is illegal to copy this book, post it to a website, or distribute it by any other means without permission.

First edition

*This book was professionally typeset on Reedsy.
Find out more at reedsy.com*

Contents

1. Chapter 1: The Anatomy of Power — 1
2. Chapter 2: The Evolution of Political Systems — 3
3. Chapter 3: The Dynamics of Social Change — 5
4. Chapter 4: The Economics of Inequality — 7
5. Chapter 5: The Role of Ideology in Society — 9
6. Chapter 6: The Interplay of Politics and Economics — 11
7. Chapter 6: The Interplay of Politics and Economics (cont'd) — 12
8. Chapter 7: The Impact of Globalization — 14
9. Chapter 8: The Role of Technology in Society — 16
10. Chapter 9: The Ethics of Economic Systems — 18
11. Chapter 10: The Politics of Identity — 20
12. Chapter 11: The Future of Democracy — 22
13. Chapter 11: The Future of Democracy (cont'd) — 24
14. Chapter 12: Towards a Just and Sustainable Future — 25

1

Chapter 1: The Anatomy of Power

In the vast expanse of human history, power has been the invisible hand that shapes societies and directs destinies. At its core, power is the ability to influence, direct, and control the actions of others. It manifests in countless ways, from the coercive power of military force to the subtle sway of cultural norms. Understanding the anatomy of power requires a deep dive into its sources, structures, and symbols. Power is not merely possessed; it is enacted, contested, and negotiated in every social interaction and political maneuver.

The sources of power are diverse, ranging from economic wealth and political authority to social status and knowledge. Economic power is wielded by those who control resources, capital, and labor, while political power resides in the ability to make and enforce laws. Social power, on the other hand, stems from one's position within social hierarchies and networks. Knowledge, often overlooked, is a potent source of power, as those who control information can shape perceptions and narratives.

The structures of power are the institutions and systems that sustain and reproduce power relations. These include governments, corporations, educational institutions, and media organizations. Each of these structures operates according to specific rules, norms, and hierarchies, which determine who has access to power and how it is exercised. However, these structures are not monolithic; they are dynamic and constantly evolving, shaped by the actions and interactions of individuals and groups.

Symbols of power, such as titles, uniforms, and insignia, serve to legitimize and reinforce power relations. They are the visible markers of authority and status, conveying messages about who is in control and who is subordinate. These symbols are not just ornamental; they play a crucial role in maintaining social order by making power visible and recognizable. Understanding these symbols is essential for decoding the complexities of power in contemporary society.

2

Chapter 2: The Evolution of Political Systems

Political systems, like living organisms, evolve over time, adapting to changing environments and challenges. The history of political systems is a chronicle of human ingenuity and resilience, marked by periods of stability and upheaval, progress and regression. From the city-states of ancient Greece to the modern nation-state, political systems have undergone profound transformations, each reflecting the values, aspirations, and conflicts of its time.

The earliest political systems were based on kinship and tribal affiliations, where leadership was often determined by age, wisdom, or martial prowess. These systems were characterized by their fluidity and adaptability, with power being decentralized and shared among multiple leaders. As societies grew larger and more complex, the need for centralized authority became more pressing, leading to the rise of monarchies and empires.

Monarchies, with their emphasis on hereditary rule and divine right, centralized power in the hands of a single ruler or ruling family. This concentration of power allowed for greater administrative efficiency and territorial expansion but also created opportunities for abuse and corruption. The fall of monarchies, often precipitated by popular revolts and internal strife, gave way to new forms of governance, such as republics and democracies.

Democratic systems, with their emphasis on popular sovereignty and representation, have become the dominant political model in the contemporary world. However, democracy is not a static or uniform concept; it varies widely in its forms and practices. From direct democracy, where citizens participate directly in decision-making, to representative democracy, where elected officials make decisions on behalf of the people, the democratic experiment continues to evolve, shaped by technological advancements, social movements, and global interdependencies.

3

Chapter 3: The Dynamics of Social Change

Society, like a living organism, is in a constant state of flux, shaped by the interplay of various forces and factors. Social change is the process by which societies transform over time, altering their structures, norms, and values. This change can be gradual or sudden, evolutionary or revolutionary, driven by a multitude of factors, including technological advancements, economic shifts, cultural movements, and political struggles. Understanding the dynamics of social change requires a multidisciplinary approach, drawing on insights from sociology, anthropology, history, and political science.

Technological advancements have been one of the primary drivers of social change throughout history. From the invention of the wheel to the rise of the internet, technology has revolutionized the way we live, work, and communicate. Each technological breakthrough has brought with it new opportunities and challenges, reshaping social relations and economic structures. The industrial revolution, for example, transformed agrarian societies into industrial powerhouses, leading to urbanization, the rise of the working class, and the spread of new political ideologies.

Economic shifts, such as the transition from feudalism to capitalism, have also played a crucial role in shaping social change. Economic systems determine how resources are distributed and who has access to wealth and power. Changes in these systems can lead to profound social transformations, as seen in the rise of the bourgeoisie and the decline of the aristocracy in the aftermath of the industrial revolution. Today, the globalized economy, with its emphasis on free markets and transnational corporations, continues to drive social change, creating new inequalities and opportunities.

Cultural movements, such as the Renaissance, the Enlightenment, and the Civil Rights Movement, have also been pivotal in shaping social change. These movements challenge existing norms and values, advocating for new ways of thinking and living. They often emerge in response to perceived injustices or crises, drawing on the collective creativity and agency of individuals and groups. While cultural movements can be disruptive, they also open up new possibilities for social innovation and progress.

4

Chapter 4: The Economics of Inequality

Inequality is a pervasive and persistent feature of human societies, manifesting in various forms, including economic, social, and political inequality. At its core, economic inequality refers to the unequal distribution of wealth, income, and resources among individuals and groups. This inequality is not just a reflection of individual differences in talent and effort; it is also the result of systemic factors, such as historical legacies, institutional biases, and market dynamics. Understanding the economics of inequality requires a critical examination of these factors and their interplay.

One of the key drivers of economic inequality is the unequal distribution of capital and assets. Those who own capital, such as land, buildings, and financial investments, can generate income and wealth through rents, dividends, and capital gains. In contrast, those who rely solely on labor for their income are more vulnerable to economic fluctuations and job insecurity. This disparity in ownership and control of capital creates a widening gap between the wealthy and the rest of the population.

Institutional biases, such as discrimination based on race, gender, and class, also contribute to economic inequality. These biases can manifest in various ways, including unequal access to education, employment, and social services. Discrimination in the labor market, for example, can result in lower wages and limited career opportunities for marginalized groups. Similarly, unequal access to quality education can perpetuate intergenerational cycles of poverty and exclusion.

Market dynamics, such as technological innovation and globalization, have also played a significant role in shaping economic inequality. Technological advancements, while driving economic growth and productivity, have also led to job displacement and wage polarization. High-skilled workers in technology-intensive industries have seen substantial wage gains, while low-skilled workers in traditional sectors have faced stagnating or declining wages. Globalization, with its emphasis on free trade and capital mobility, has created new opportunities for some but has also exposed many to economic volatility and competition.

5

Chapter 5: The Role of Ideology in Society

Ideology is a set of beliefs, values, and ideas that shape our understanding of the world and guide our actions. It serves as a lens through which we interpret social reality, making sense of complex phenomena and providing a framework for political and social action. Ideologies are not merely abstract theories; they are deeply embedded in our everyday lives, influencing our attitudes, behaviors, and institutions. The role of ideology in society is multifaceted, encompassing both the power to inspire and the potential to constrain.

Ideologies often emerge in response to specific historical and social contexts, reflecting the aspirations and grievances of particular groups. For example, liberalism, with its emphasis on individual rights and freedoms, emerged in the context of the Enlightenment and the struggles against absolutist monarchies. Similarly, socialism, with its critique of capitalism and advocacy for social equality, arose in response to the inequalities and injustices of the industrial revolution. These ideologies provide a coherent set of principles and goals, mobilizing individuals and groups to pursue social change.

However, ideologies can also serve as instruments of power and control, used by dominant groups to legitimize and maintain their authority. By shaping our perceptions of what is natural, just, and possible, ideologies can constrain our thinking and limit our actions. For example, the ideology of meritocracy, which emphasizes individual effort and talent as the basis for success, can obscure the structural barriers and inequalities that limit opportunities for many. Similarly, nationalist ideologies can be used to justify exclusion and aggression, perpetuating cycles of conflict and division.

Despite their potential to constrain, ideologies also have the power to inspire and empower. They provide a sense of purpose and direction, helping individuals and groups to navigate the complexities and uncertainties of social life. Ideologies can foster solidarity and collective action, enabling people to challenge injustices and envision alternative futures. In this sense, ideologies are not just passive reflections of social reality; they are active forces that shape and transform the world.

6

Chapter 6: The Interplay of Politics and Economics

The relationship between politics and economics is complex and dynamic, characterized by mutual influence and interdependence. Political decisions and institutions shape economic policies and outcomes, while economic conditions and interests influence political processes and power relations. Understanding the interplay of politics and economics requires a holistic approach, considering both the structural and agency dimensions of this relationship.

Political institutions, such as governments, parliaments, and regulatory bodies, play a crucial role in shaping economic policies

continue

7

Chapter 6: The Interplay of Politics and Economics (cont'd)

Political institutions, such as governments, parliaments, and regulatory bodies, play a crucial role in shaping economic policies and outcomes. These institutions establish the rules and regulations that govern economic activities, such as taxation, trade, labor relations, and property rights. Political decisions about public spending, monetary policy, and social welfare can significantly impact economic growth, distribution of wealth, and overall social well-being.

Economic conditions, such as inflation, unemployment, and economic growth, influence political processes and power relations. Economic crises, for example, can lead to political instability, social unrest, and changes in leadership. Economic interests, represented by various actors such as businesses, labor unions, and consumer groups, also shape political agendas and decisions. These actors use their resources and influence to lobby for policies that favor their interests, contributing to the complex interplay between politics and economics.

The relationship between politics and economics is also shaped by broader historical and cultural contexts. Historical legacies, such as colonialism, industrialization, and globalization, have left lasting imprints on political and economic structures. Cultural values and norms, such as beliefs about individualism, collectivism, and the role of the state, influence how political and economic systems are perceived and practiced. Understanding the interplay of politics and economics requires a nuanced and contextual approach, considering both the material and ideational dimensions of this relationship.

8

Chapter 7: The Impact of Globalization

Globalization is the process by which the world becomes increasingly interconnected and interdependent, driven by advances in technology, communication, and transportation. This process has profound implications for politics, society, and economics, reshaping the way we live, work, and interact. The impact of globalization is multifaceted, encompassing both opportunities and challenges, benefits and costs.

One of the key impacts of globalization is the increased flow of goods, services, and capital across borders. This has led to the growth of international trade, investment, and economic integration, creating new opportunities for economic growth and development. However, globalization has also created new inequalities and vulnerabilities, as not all countries and communities benefit equally from these processes. The global economy is marked by uneven development, with wealth and power concentrated in certain regions and sectors.

Globalization has also facilitated the spread of ideas, cultures, and technologies, leading to greater cultural diversity and exchange. This cultural globalization can foster greater understanding and cooperation among different societies but can also lead to tensions and conflicts. The spread of dominant cultures and values, often driven by powerful media and corporations, can threaten local traditions and identities, leading to cultural homogenization and resistance.

CHAPTER 7: THE IMPACT OF GLOBALIZATION

The political implications of globalization are also significant, as it challenges traditional notions of sovereignty and governance. Global issues such as climate change, terrorism, and pandemics require coordinated responses that transcend national boundaries. This has led to the rise of international organizations and agreements, as well as new forms of global governance. However, globalization also raises questions about accountability, representation, and democratic legitimacy, as decisions made at the global level can impact local communities in profound ways.

Chapter 8: The Role of Technology in Society

Technology is a driving force of social change, shaping the way we live, work, and interact. The impact of technology on society is profound and multifaceted, encompassing both opportunities and challenges, benefits and costs. Understanding the role of technology in society requires a critical examination of its historical development, current applications, and future possibilities.

The historical development of technology is a story of human ingenuity and innovation, marked by significant milestones such as the invention of the wheel, the printing press, and the internet. Each technological breakthrough has transformed societies in profound ways, creating new opportunities for economic growth, social progress, and cultural exchange. However, technological advancements have also created new challenges and dilemmas, such as environmental degradation, job displacement, and ethical concerns.

The current applications of technology are diverse and far-reaching, affecting various aspects of our lives, from communication and transportation to healthcare and education. Digital technologies, such as the internet, social media, and mobile devices, have revolutionized the way we communicate and access information. These technologies have created new opportunities for social connectivity, civic engagement, and economic innovation, but they

CHAPTER 8: THE ROLE OF TECHNOLOGY IN SOCIETY

have also raised concerns about privacy, security, and the digital divide.

The future possibilities of technology are both exciting and uncertain, as emerging technologies such as artificial intelligence, biotechnology, and quantum computing hold the potential to transform societies in unprecedented ways. These technologies promise to revolutionize various fields, from medicine and agriculture to energy and transportation, creating new opportunities for progress and development. However, they also raise important ethical and social questions, such as the implications of automation for employment, the risks of biotechnological interventions, and the governance of advanced technologies.

10

Chapter 9: The Ethics of Economic Systems

Economic systems are not just mechanisms for producing and distributing goods and services; they are also moral and ethical frameworks that reflect and shape our values, priorities, and aspirations. The ethics of economic systems encompass a range of questions and dilemmas, such as the distribution of wealth and income, the role of markets and the state, and the balance between efficiency and equity. Understanding the ethics of economic systems requires a critical examination of these questions and their implications for individuals and societies.

One of the key ethical questions in economic systems is the distribution of wealth and income. Economic inequality raises important moral concerns, such as fairness, justice, and social cohesion. While some argue that inequality is a natural and inevitable outcome of market processes and individual differences in talent and effort, others contend that it reflects and perpetuates structural injustices and power imbalances. Addressing economic inequality requires not only economic policies but also ethical reflection and social action.

The role of markets and the state in economic systems is another important ethical question. Markets are often praised for their efficiency and dynamism, as they allocate resources based on supply and demand and encourage

CHAPTER 9: THE ETHICS OF ECONOMIC SYSTEMS

innovation and competition. However, markets can also lead to negative outcomes, such as monopolies, externalities, and inequalities. The state, as a political and social institution, has a responsibility to regulate and complement markets, ensuring that economic activities serve the public good and protect vulnerable individuals and communities.

The balance between efficiency and equity is a central ethical dilemma in economic systems. Efficiency refers to the optimal allocation of resources to maximize productivity and growth, while equity refers to the fair distribution of resources and opportunities. Striking a balance between these goals requires careful consideration of both the material and moral dimensions of economic systems, recognizing that efficiency without equity can lead to social fragmentation and injustice, while equity without efficiency can undermine economic sustainability and progress.

11

Chapter 10: The Politics of Identity

Identity is a fundamental aspect of human existence, shaping our sense of self, our relationships with others, and our place in the world. The politics of identity refers to the ways in which identities are constructed, expressed, and contested in social and political contexts. It encompasses a range of issues, such as race, gender, sexuality, nationality, and religion, and their intersections. Understanding the politics of identity requires a critical examination of the processes and power dynamics that shape identities and their implications for individuals and societies.

Identities are not fixed or given; they are constructed through social and historical processes, shaped by cultural norms, institutional practices, and individual experiences. The construction of identities involves both inclusion and exclusion, as it defines who belongs and who does not, who is privileged and who is marginalized. This process is often contested, as different groups and individuals seek to assert their identities and challenge dominant narratives and hierarchies.

The expression of identities is a dynamic and multifaceted process, encompassing various forms of cultural, social, and political practices. From artistic expressions and cultural performances to social movements and political activism, individuals and groups use various means to express and affirm their identities. These expressions can foster a sense of belonging, solidarity, and empowerment, but they can also lead to tensions and conflicts, as different

CHAPTER 10: THE POLITICS OF IDENTITY

identities and interests collide.

The politics of identity is also shaped by broader social, political, and economic contexts. Historical legacies, such as colonialism, slavery, and patriarchy, have left lasting imprints on identity politics, shaping power relations and social inequalities. Contemporary challenges, such as migration, globalization, and technological change, further complicate the politics of identity, creating new opportunities and dilemmas. Understanding the politics of identity requires a nuanced and contextual approach, recognizing the diversity and complexity of identities and their intersections.

12

Chapter 11: The Future of Democracy

Democracy, as a political system and ideal, has evolved over time, reflecting the aspirations and struggles of individuals and societies. The future of democracy is a topic of ongoing debate and speculation, as it faces both opportunities and challenges in the contemporary world. Understanding the future of democracy requires a critical examination of its historical development, current practices, and future possibilities.

The historical development of democracy is a story of human ingenuity and resilience, marked by periods of progress and regression, innovation and adaptation. From the direct democracies of ancient Greece to the representative democracies of the modern world, democracy has evolved in response to changing social, political, and economic conditions. This evolution has been shaped by various factors, such as technological advancements, social movements, and global interdependencies, which have influenced the forms and practices of democracy.

Current practices of democracy vary widely, reflecting the diversity of political systems and cultures around the world. While some democracies are characterized by strong institutions, vibrant civil societies, and inclusive participation, others face significant challenges, such as political polarization, corruption, and democratic backsliding. These challenges highlight the need for ongoing efforts to strengthen and renew democratic practices, ensuring that they are responsive to the needs and aspirations of individuals and

CHAPTER 11: THE FUTURE OF DEMOCRACY

communities.

The future possibilities of democracy are both exciting and uncertain, as emerging technologies, social movements, and global challenges create new opportunities and dilemmas. Technological advancements, such as artificial intelligence and digital platforms, hold the potential to enhance democratic participation and transparency but also raise concerns about privacy,
  continue

13

Chapter 11: The Future of Democracy (cont'd)

... but also raise concerns about privacy, misinformation, and the concentration of power in digital platforms. Addressing these concerns requires new forms of regulation, oversight, and civic engagement, ensuring that technological advancements serve the public good and enhance democratic values.

Social movements, such as those advocating for racial justice, climate action, and gender equality, hold the potential to renew and transform democratic practices. These movements challenge existing power structures and advocate for more inclusive and participatory forms of democracy. They demonstrate the power of collective action and the importance of grassroots organizing in shaping political agendas and outcomes.

Global challenges, such as climate change, migration, and economic inequality, also pose significant tests for the future of democracy. Addressing these challenges requires coordinated and collaborative responses that transcend national boundaries and involve diverse stakeholders. This necessitates new forms of global governance and cooperation, as well as a renewed commitment to democratic principles and values.

14

Chapter 12: Towards a Just and Sustainable Future

The quest for a just and sustainable future is one of the defining challenges of our time. It requires a holistic approach that integrates social, economic, and environmental dimensions, recognizing their interconnections and interdependencies. Achieving this vision necessitates transformative changes in our political, economic, and social systems, guided by principles of justice, equity, and sustainability.

Justice is a fundamental principle that underpins our vision of a better future. It demands that we address the root causes of inequality and injustice, ensuring that all individuals and communities have access to the resources and opportunities they need to thrive. This requires not only redistributive policies but also structural reforms that challenge existing power relations and create more inclusive and equitable institutions.

Sustainability is another key principle, emphasizing the need to balance economic growth with environmental stewardship and social well-being. This requires a shift towards more sustainable forms of production and consumption, reducing our ecological footprint and preserving the planet's resources for future generations. It also demands a recognition of the interconnectedness of social and environmental issues, addressing the ways in which environmental degradation disproportionately affects marginalized communities.

Achieving a just and sustainable future also requires a commitment to democratic values and practices, ensuring that all individuals have a voice in the decisions that affect their lives. This involves not only formal democratic institutions but also vibrant civil societies, inclusive participatory processes, and a culture of active citizenship. It demands that we foster a sense of shared responsibility and solidarity, recognizing our collective agency in shaping our common future.

In conclusion, the quest for a just and sustainable future is a complex and multifaceted challenge that requires bold and visionary leadership, innovative solutions, and collective action. It calls for a reimagining of our political, economic, and social systems, guided by principles of justice, equity, and sustainability. By embracing these principles and working together, we can create a future that is not only more just and equitable but also more resilient and sustainable.

Book Description:

The Human Algorithm: Decoding Politics, Society, and Economics in the Modern World is an insightful exploration into the intricate dynamics that shape our lives today. This book delves into the anatomy of power, the evolution of political systems, the dynamics of social change, and the economics of inequality. Each chapter unravels the complexities of how our societies are organized and governed, revealing the underlying forces that drive change and continuity.

From the origins of political power to the impacts of globalization and technological advancements, this book examines the multifaceted interactions between politics, economics, and society. It provides a comprehensive analysis of how ideologies shape our worldviews, the interplay between politics and economics, and the ethical considerations that underpin economic systems.

Through a critical and engaging lens, **The Human Algorithm** also addresses contemporary issues such as the politics of identity, the future of democracy, and the quest for a just and sustainable future. It offers a nuanced understanding of the challenges and opportunities that lie ahead,

CHAPTER 12: TOWARDS A JUST AND SUSTAINABLE FUTURE

advocating for transformative changes that prioritize justice, equity, and sustainability.

Whether you are a student of social sciences, a policy-maker, or simply a curious reader, this book is an invaluable resource for understanding the complex world we live in. It invites you to reflect on the principles and practices that shape our societies and envision a future that is more inclusive, equitable, and resilient.